W9-AOW-027

GRAPHIC FORENSIC SCIENCE

CORPSES AND SKELETONS:

THE SCIENCE OF FORENSIC ANTHROPOLOGY

by Rob Shone

illustrated by Nick Spender

Rosen
Classroom

Published in 2008 by The Rosen Publishing Group, Inc.
29 East 21st Street, New York, NY 10010

First edition, 2008

Designed and produced by
David West Books

Editor: Gail Bushnell

Photo credits:
P4/5, istockphoto.com/Chris Ronneseth; 6t, U.S. National Library of Medicine; 6b, istockphoto.com/Clayton Hansen; 7t, U.S. National Library of Medicine; 7b, istockphoto.com/Jaroslaw Wojcik; 44t, istockphoto.com/Nikola Bilic; 45t, istockphoto/Torbjorn Lagerwall.

Library of Congress Cataloging-in-Publication Data

Shone, Rob.
  Corpses and skeletons : the science of forensic anthropology / by
Rob Shone ; illustrated by Nick Spender. -- 1st ed.
      p. cm. -- (Graphic forensic science)
  Includes index.
  ISBN 978-1-4042-1440-8 (library binding) -- ISBN 978-1-4042-1441-5
(pbk.) -- ISBN 978-1-4042-1442-2 (6 pack)
  1. Forensic anthropology--Juvenile literature. I. Spender, Nik,
ill. II. Title.
  GN69.8.S56 2008
  614'.17--dc22

                                        2007041763

CONTENTS

THE CRIME SCENE

Human bones are often unearthed. They can be found on building sites, in plowed fields, and in fact anywhere the ground has been disturbed. Most are old, and are of interest only to archaeologists. Some bones, however, belong to the victims of murder.

THE SIGNS OF MURDER

When a crime scene has been identified it is quickly made secure. Only a few people are allowed onto the scene, so evidence will not be damaged. Most of the evidence is collected by the crime scene investigators (CSI). They make careful records of everything they see. The crime scene, and every piece of evidence, is photographed and drawn. Some forensic experts work alongside the CSI at this point. Any bones that are found are examined by a forensic anthropologist while still at the scene. The anthropologist will also study them more closely in a laboratory. Another expert who might be there is the forensic entomologist. Insect samples would have to be collected from the scene as soon as possible.

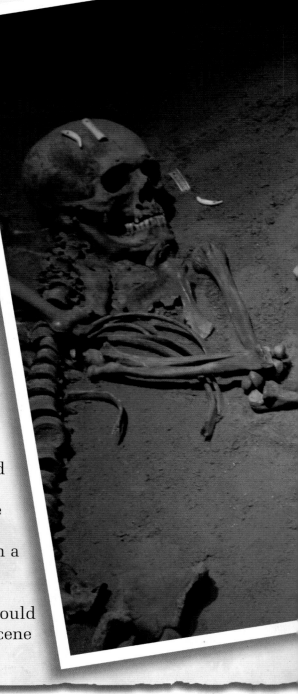

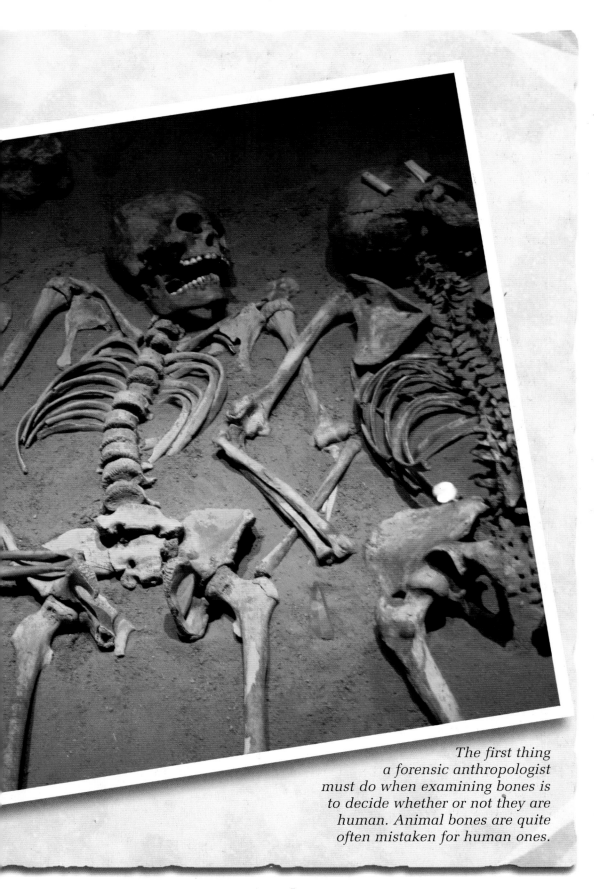

The first thing a forensic anthropologist must do when examining bones is to decide whether or not they are human. Animal bones are quite often mistaken for human ones.

BODIES, BUGS, AND BONES

There are 206 bones in the human body. A forensic anthropologist must be able to recognize them all.

A dead body can turn into a skeleton in less than a month if the conditions are right. When a body has decomposed that much, normal detective work can be difficult. The police may have to rely on the experts for help.

FORENSIC ANTHROPOLOGY

Forensic anthropologists study the human skeleton. Their main job is to identify bodies. Just a few bones can tell them a great deal. A thighbone or upper arm bone can give a height for the body. The thighbone can also tell the anthropologist the sex of the skeleton, as can the skull, hip bone, and teeth. These bones are different in men and women. As people grow older some of their bones change. This makes it possible to know the age of a skeleton. Forensic anthropologists also look for damage to bones. Marks made by knives, bullets, or a blunt instrument can indicate how a person died. Signs of bone disease and bone wear might provide information about how a person lived.

The forensic anthropologist often works with a forensic odontologist (dentist). Using X-rays, they will try to match a skeleton to its dental records.

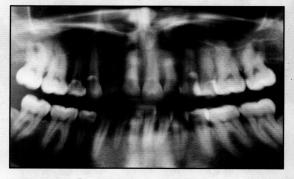

ART AND FORENSICS

While the forensic anthropologist can tell what a skeleton looked like when it was alive, the forensic artist can give the skeleton a face. This may help identify John and Jane Does (unidentified bodies). The forensic artist can also help solve cold cases, old crimes that are reexamined. The faces of people who have been missing for years can be drawn to show them looking older.

Knowing how the face muscles are arranged is vital if the forensic artist is to create a lifelike reconstruction.

FORENSIC ENTOMOLOGY

Entomology is the study of insects. In criminal cases they are generally used to find the time of death of a murder victim. Many different types of insect will infest a dead body. They appear on the corpse in a particular order and after a set amount of time. Knowing this timetable allows the entomologist to work back and discover when the person died. Insects can be useful to the criminalist in other ways. Some are only found in specific areas. So if those bugs are found on the windshield or grille of a suspect's car, the entomologist will know where that car has recently been.

Maggots may not be pretty to look at, but they are important to the forensic entomologist in finding a murder victim's time of death.

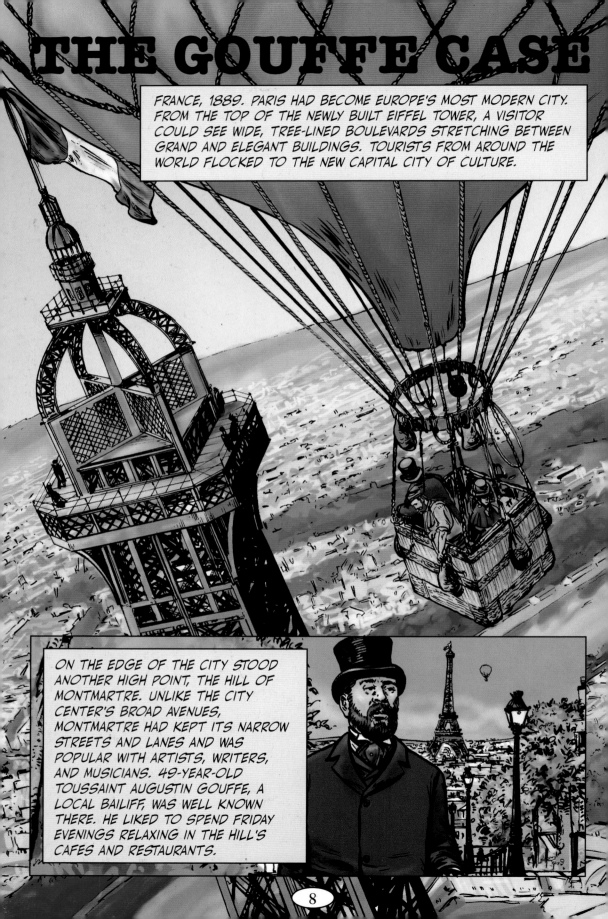

THE GOUFFE CASE

FRANCE, 1889. PARIS HAD BECOME EUROPE'S MOST MODERN CITY. FROM THE TOP OF THE NEWLY BUILT EIFFEL TOWER, A VISITOR COULD SEE WIDE, TREE-LINED BOULEVARDS STRETCHING BETWEEN GRAND AND ELEGANT BUILDINGS. TOURISTS FROM AROUND THE WORLD FLOCKED TO THE NEW CAPITAL CITY OF CULTURE.

ON THE EDGE OF THE CITY STOOD ANOTHER HIGH POINT, THE HILL OF MONTMARTRE. UNLIKE THE CITY CENTER'S BROAD AVENUES, MONTMARTRE HAD KEPT ITS NARROW STREETS AND LANES AND WAS POPULAR WITH ARTISTS, WRITERS, AND MUSICIANS. 49-YEAR-OLD TOUSSAINT AUGUSTIN GOUFFE, A LOCAL BAILIFF, WAS WELL KNOWN THERE. HE LIKED TO SPEND FRIDAY EVENINGS RELAXING IN THE HILL'S CAFES AND RESTAURANTS.

FRIDAY, JULY 26, WAS NO DIFFERENT. AFTER CLOSING HIS OFFICE, THE BAILIFF MET WITH SOME OF HIS FRIENDS.

IS YOUR KNEE GIVING YOU TROUBLE AGAIN?

OOF! SLOW DOWN. I CAN'T WALK AS QUICKLY AS YOU TWO, REMEMBER.

THE WHOLE LEG ACHES TODAY.

WE'RE GOING TO THE MOULIN GALETTE FOR DINNER LATER ON. WHY DON'T YOU COME ALONG, TOUSSAINT?

JUST AFTER SEVEN O'CLOCK GOUFFE SAID GOOD-BYE TO HIS FRIENDS AND LEFT THEM. THEY NEVER SAW HIM AGAIN.

I'D LIKE TO, BUT I ALREADY HAVE DINNER PLANS.

SUNDAY, JULY 28. INSPECTOR GORON AND HIS ASSISTANT, SERGEANT JAUME, WERE AT TOUSSAINT GOUFFE'S OFFICE IN THE RUE MONTMARTRE. HE HAD NOT BEEN SEEN SINCE FRIDAY AND THE POLICE WERE INVESTIGATING THE DISAPPEARANCE.

WELL, WHAT HAVE YOU FOUND, JAUME?

SOMEONE WAS HERE BEFORE US, SIR, THE ROOM'S BEEN SEARCHED. WHOEVER IT WAS DIDN'T FIND THIS, THOUGH.

THERE MUST BE THOUSANDS OF FRANCS HERE!

YES, FOURTEEN THOUSAND—I COUNTED THEM. IT WAS LYING UNDER A PILE OF PAPERS. THE INTRUDER MISSED IT.

HMM. THERE ARE BURNT MATCHES ON THE FLOOR. DID ANYONE SEE THE INTRUDER?

THE HALL PORTER HEARD SOMEONE COME UP THE STAIRS TO THE OFFICE AT AROUND NINE O'CLOCK.

HE THOUGHT IT WAS GOUFFE AT FIRST. WHEN THE INTRUDER LEFT A FEW MINUTES LATER, HE SAW THAT IT WASN'T.

DID THE PORTER SEE HIS FACE?

NO, IT WAS TOO DARK.

NEWS OF THE DISCOVERY REACHED INSPECTOR GORON. HE SENT JAUME AND GOUFFE'S BROTHER-IN-LAW TO IDENTIFY THE BODY.

GASP!

I SHOULD HAVE WARNED YOU. THEY DON'T LOOK SO PRETTY AFTER A FEW WEEKS OUTSIDE IN THIS HEAT.

OUTSIDE... TAKE A DEEP BREATH, SIR. YOU'LL FEEL BETTER IN A MINUTE OR TWO.

BY THE FALL, THE CASE SEEMED TO BE AT A DEAD END UNTIL, BY CHANCE, GORON MET ONE OF GOUFFE'S FRIENDS...

DON'T YOU THINK IT STRANGE THAT TWO PEOPLE FROM THE SAME PART OF PARIS SHOULD GO MISSING AT THE SAME TIME, INSPECTOR?

I'M SORRY, IT WAS A BIT OF A SHOCK. IT'S NOT MY BROTHER-IN-LAW. THAT—THING—HAS BLACK HAIR. TOUSSAINT'S IS BROWN.

A "SECOND" PERSON? WHO?

MICHEL EYRAUD WAS 46 YEARS OF AGE. EYRAUD'S BUSINESS HAD RECENTLY FAILED AND HE WAS THOUSANDS OF FRANCS IN DEBT. INSPECTOR GORON LEARNED THAT HE HAD LEFT PARIS THE DAY AFTER GOUFFE'S DISAPPEARANCE, ALONG WITH A FRIEND, TWENTY-ONE-YEAR-OLD GABRIELLE BOMPARD.

SOON ANOTHER BREAKTHROUGH WAS MADE. A SMASHED TRUNK HAD BEEN FOUND IN THE SAME WOOD AS THE BODY. AT GARE DE LYON, PARIS– THE RAILWAY STATION THAT SERVED THE SOUTHEAST OF FRANCE...

THE POLICE IN LYON DIDN'T LINK THE TRUNK TO THE CRIME AT FIRST, JAUME. IT WAS FOUND NOWHERE NEAR THE BODY AND A RAILWAY LABEL ON IT WAS DATED "1888."

BUT THEN A KEY FOUND CLOSE TO THE BODY FITTED THE TRUNK'S LOCK. AND THE DATE ON THE LABEL IS SMUDGED AND NOT EASY TO READ.

THE RAILWAY RECORDS OFFICE...

HERE IT IS! THE TRUNK, WEIGHING 230 POUNDS, WAS PUT ON A TRAIN BOUND FOR LYON...

...ON JULY 27, **1889**, THE DAY AFTER GOUFFE'S DISAPPEARANCE. THE BODY IN LYON IS FROM PARIS.

13

IN NOVEMBER INSPECTOR GORON WENT TO LYON AND HAD THE MYSTERY BODY DUG UP FROM ITS GRAVE.

HE HAD ARRANGED FOR DR. LACASSAGNE FROM THE LYON SCHOOL OF FORENSIC MEDICINE TO PERFORM A NEW AUTOPSY.

DON'T YOU WANT TO GET A CLOSER LOOK, JAUME?

I'VE ALREADY SEEN ENOUGH OF THE BODY, SIR. BESIDES, IT'S LITTLE MORE THAN A SKELETON...

...WHAT CAN LACASSAGNE TELL US FROM THAT?

LOOKING AT THE PELVIS, I CAN SEE THAT IT IS MALE. THE FEMALE PELVIS IS SLIGHTLY WIDER.

FROM THE WEAR ON HIS TEETH, I WOULD SAY HE WAS BETWEEN FORTY-FIVE AND FIFTY YEARS OLD.

BY MEASURING THE THIGH AND UPPER ARM BONES I CAN TELL HOW TALL HE WAS.

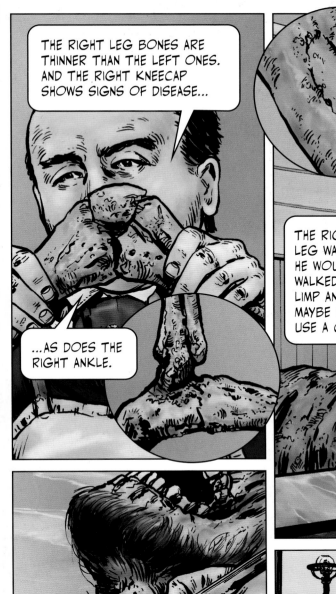

THE RIGHT LEG BONES ARE THINNER THAN THE LEFT ONES. AND THE RIGHT KNEECAP SHOWS SIGNS OF DISEASE...

...AS DOES THE RIGHT ANKLE.

THE SCARRING ON THE THIGHBONE WHERE THE MUSCLES WERE ATTACHED IS SMALLER THAN ON THE LEFT LEG.

THE RIGHT LEG WAS WEAK. HE WOULD HAVE WALKED WITH A LIMP AND MAYBE HAD TO USE A CANE.

AH! AS FOR HOW HE DIED, LOOK AT THIS! SEE, THE THYROID CARTILAGE HAS BEEN BROKEN.

SUCH AN INJURY CAN ONLY MEAN THAT HE WAS STRANGLED TO DEATH, INSPECTOR.

15

IT STILL CAN'T BE GOUFFE, THOUGH. THE HAIR IS THE WRONG COLOR.

THE HAIR HAS BEEN DYED. ITS REAL COLOR IS BROWN.

REALLY? COULD YOU PASS ME THAT BOWL OF WATER, PLEASE?

I PRESENT TO YOU MR. TOUSSAINT AUGUSTIN GOUFFE.

SO, WE KNOW WHO THE VICTIM IS. ALL WE HAVE TO DO NOW IS CONNECT THE TRUNK TO EYRAUD AND BOMPARD, AND WE'VE SOLVED THE CRIME.

BACK IN PARIS, GORON HAD A REPLICA OF THE TRUNK PUT ON DISPLAY. THE EFFORT PAID OFF. A HOTEL OWNER FROM LONDON WAS IN PARIS AT THE TIME...

I'VE SEEN THAT TRUNK BEFORE! I MUST LET THE POLICE KNOW.

HE REMEMBERED THAT A TRUNK, EXACTLY LIKE THE ONE ON SHOW, HAD BEEN BOUGHT IN ENGLAND BY A FRENCH COUPLE WHO WERE STAYING AT HIS HOTEL.

THEY WERE MICHEL EYRAUD AND GABRIELLE BOMPARD. WE HAVE THEM, JAUME!

WARRANTS FOR THEIR ARREST WERE ISSUED. BEFORE SHE COULD BE CAUGHT, BOMPARD GAVE HERSELF UP.

AH, INSPECTOR GORON, I UNDERSTAND YOU'RE LOOKING FOR ME.

SHE BLAMED EYRAUD FOR THE MURDER.

BUT INSPECTOR, YOU MUST BELIEVE ME, IT WAS ALL EYRAUD'S IDEA! HE TRICKED ME INTO HELPING HIM!

LOCK HER UP.

EYRAUD HAD FLED FROM FRANCE. IN JUNE 1890, HE WAS EVENTUALLY CAUGHT IN HAVANA, CUBA.

WHEN GORON CONFRONTED THE PAIR WITH THE EVIDENCE, THEY CONFESSED. AT LAST THE INSPECTOR KNEW THE WHOLE STORY.

THE KILLERS HAD CHOSEN GOUFFE CAREFULLY. EYRAUD WAS IN FINANCIAL TROUBLE AND KNEW THE BAILIFF CARRIED LARGE AMOUNTS OF MONEY AROUND WITH HIM.

BOMPARD HAD MADE FRIENDS WITH GOUFFE AND INVITED HIM TO HER APARTMENT...

AT ABOUT EIGHT O'CLOCK BOMPARD TOOK GOUFFE HOME WITH HER.

IS IT FAR, DEAR? ONLY— IT'S MY KNEE, YOU SEE...

NO, JUST A LITTLE FARTHER.

LATER...

WHY DON'T YOU SIT OVER THERE ON THE COUCH WHILE I GET SOME WINE?

THEY WERE NOT ALONE IN THE ROOM. MICHEL EYRAUD WAS ALSO THERE...

...HIDING.

GOUFFE WAS ENJOYING BOMPARD'S COMPANY.

A CURTAIN CORD TIE WOULD MAKE YOU LOOK SO HANDSOME, TOUSSAINT.

SUDDENLY...

NOW YOU'RE MAKING FUN OF ME, MISS BOMPARD.

IN A FLASH, EYRAUD HAD GRABBED THE CORD, TIED IT TO A ROPE AND PULLEY...

...AND HEAVED.

19

AFTER A FEW MINUTES GOUFFE WAS DEAD. THEY DID NOT KNOW THAT ON FRIDAYS, HE LEFT THE DAY'S TAKINGS IN HIS OFFICE.

IS THIS ALL HE HAD? ONE HUNDRED AND FIFTY FRANCS*?

I DON'T UNDERSTAND. NORMALLY HE CARRIES THOUSANDS! IT MUST ALL BE AT HIS OFFICE.

*IN 1889 A COMMON LABORER IN PARIS EARNED ABOUT FOUR FRANCS A DAY.

EYRAUD RUSHED TO GOUFFE'S OFFICE IN THE RUE MONTMARTRE.

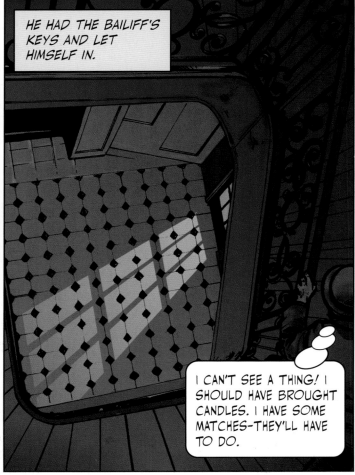

HE HAD THE BAILIFF'S KEYS AND LET HIMSELF IN.

I CAN'T SEE A THING! I SHOULD HAVE BROUGHT CANDLES. I HAVE SOME MATCHES—THEY'LL HAVE TO DO.

WHEN HE HAD USED ALL HIS MATCHES HE LEFT—WITHOUT FINDING THE HIDDEN 14,000 FRANCS.

ON HIS WAY OUT HE WAS SEEN BY THE PORTER.

HEY! WHO ARE YOU? WHAT DO YOU WANT?

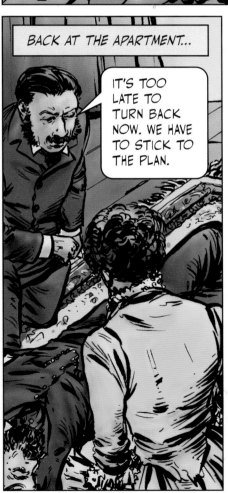

BACK AT THE APARTMENT...

IT'S TOO LATE TO TURN BACK NOW. WE HAVE TO STICK TO THE PLAN.

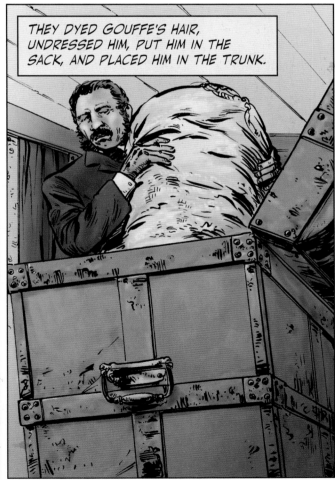

THEY DYED GOUFFE'S HAIR, UNDRESSED HIM, PUT HIM IN THE SACK, AND PLACED HIM IN THE TRUNK.

THE FOLLOWING DAY THE KILLERS CAUGHT THE TRAIN TO LYON. IN A WOOD JUST OUTSIDE THE CITY...

EYRAUD TOOK THE TRUNK TO A DIFFERENT PART OF THE WOOD AND SMASHED IT SO THAT IT WOULD NOT BE CONNECTED TO THE CRIME. THE BODY WAS LEFT IN THE PLACE WHERE IT WAS FOUND TWO WEEKS LATER.

ON DECEMBER 16, 1890, THE TRIAL OF MICHEL EYRAUD AND GABRIELLE BOMPARD BEGAN. FIVE DAYS LATER IT WAS OVER. BOMPARD WAS SENTENCED TO 20 YEARS IN PRISON.

MICHEL EYRAUD, YOU HAVE BEEN FOUND GUILTY OF MURDER. THE SENTENCE OF THE COURT IS DEATH.

BODY IN THE CARPET

10:30 P.M., SEPTEMBER 21, 1986, INTERSTATE 95, GREENWICH, CONNECTICUT. THE POLICE HAD BEEN WAITING FOR THE MEDICAL EXAMINER TO ARRIVE. NOW THAT HE WAS THERE THEY COULD CONTINUE.

HAS ANYONE TOUCHED IT?

ONLY THE GUY WHO FOUND IT. THAT'S HOW WE KNOW THERE'S A BODY WRAPPED INSIDE.

IT'S FEMALE AND BEEN DEAD FOR SOME TIME, I'D SAY.

HELP ME UNROLL IT.

WE'RE NOT GOING TO GET A TIME OF DEATH OUT OF HER—SHE'S BEEN HERE TOO LONG TO USE THE NORMAL MARKERS. THIS IS ONE FOR THE BUG DETECTIVES.

MAGGOTS AND INSECTS WERE COLLECTED FROM THE BODY. SOME WERE KILLED, OTHERS WERE KEPT ALIVE.

THE SAMPLES WERE SENT TO DR. WILLIAM KRINSKY AT YALE UNIVERSITY, NEW HAVEN, CONNECTICUT. MEANWHILE, THE POLICE HAD FOUND OUT THAT THE BODY BELONGED TO 26-YEAR-OLD SYLVIA HUNT. SHE HAD BEEN STABBED TO DEATH.

GOOD, THEY'VE SENT LIVE BLOWFLY MAGGOTS AND PUPAE*.

*SEE PAGE 29.

WHAT'S SO SPECIAL ABOUT BLOWFLIES? TO ME A FLY IS JUST A FLY.

THESE HAVE A VERY PREDICTABLE LIFE CYCLE, OFFICER.

WE KNOW HOW LONG EACH STAGE OF THEIR DEVELOPMENT TAKES.

DR. KRINSKY PLACED BLOWFLY PUPAE FROM THE CRIME SCENE IN A HATCHING BOX AND KEPT IT AT 77°F (25°C).

THEY'RE USUALLY THE FIRST INSECT ON THE SCENE WHENEVER THERE'S A BODY AROUND.

WHEN THEY HATCH I'LL BE ABLE TO FIGURE OUT WHEN THE EGGS WERE LAID. THE BODY MUST HAVE DIED NOT LONG BEFORE THAT TIME.

AN ADULT BLOWFLY HAS AN EXCELLENT SENSE OF SMELL...

...AND CAN TRACK DOWN A CORPSE JUST MINUTES OLD.

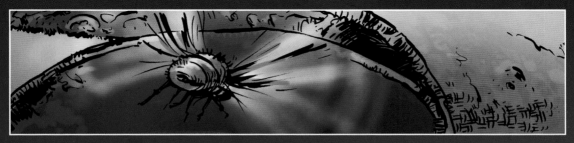

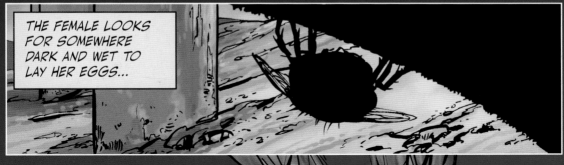

THE FEMALE LOOKS FOR SOMEWHERE DARK AND WET TO LAY HER EGGS...

...EITHER IN A NATURAL BODY OPENING...

...OR IN A FRESH WOUND.

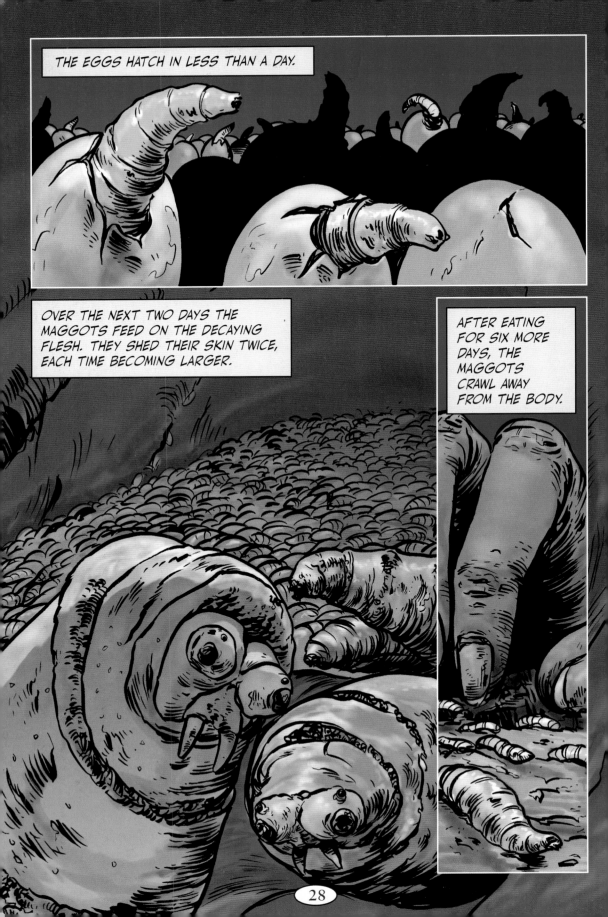

THE EGGS HATCH IN LESS THAN A DAY.

OVER THE NEXT TWO DAYS THE MAGGOTS FEED ON THE DECAYING FLESH. THEY SHED THEIR SKIN TWICE, EACH TIME BECOMING LARGER.

AFTER EATING FOR SIX MORE DAYS, THE MAGGOTS CRAWL AWAY FROM THE BODY.

THEY BECOME SHORT AND FAT AS THEIR SKIN HARDENS AND THEY TURN INTO PUPAE.

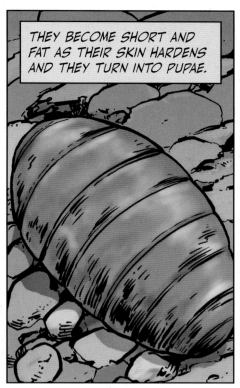

INSIDE ITS HARD CASE THE MAGGOT TAKES SIX DAYS TO CHANGE INTO AN ADULT BLOWFLY...

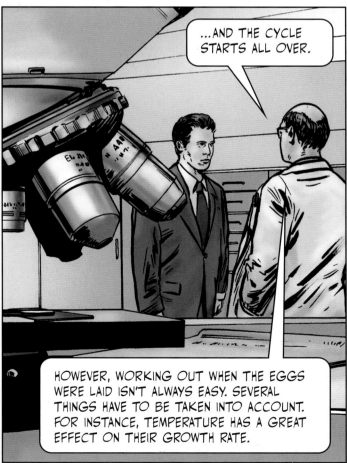

...AND THE CYCLE STARTS ALL OVER.

HOWEVER, WORKING OUT WHEN THE EGGS WERE LAID ISN'T ALWAYS EASY. SEVERAL THINGS HAVE TO BE TAKEN INTO ACCOUNT. FOR INSTANCE, TEMPERATURE HAS A GREAT EFFECT ON THEIR GROWTH RATE.

IT SLOWS DOWN IN COLD WEATHER, WHICH MEANS THAT THE EGGS MAY HAVE BEEN LAID EARLIER THAN FIRST THOUGHT.

SO I HAVE TO CHECK THE LOCAL WEATHER REPORTS TO SEE HOW WARM OR COLD IT'S BEEN.

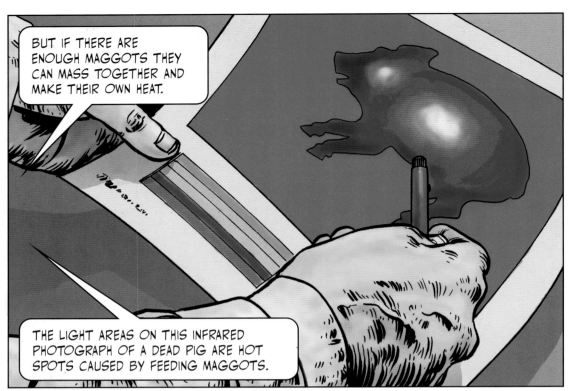

BUT IF THERE ARE ENOUGH MAGGOTS THEY CAN MASS TOGETHER AND MAKE THEIR OWN HEAT.

THE LIGHT AREAS ON THIS INFRARED PHOTOGRAPH OF A DEAD PIG ARE HOT SPOTS CAUSED BY FEEDING MAGGOTS.

THE GROWTH RATE CAN BE NORMAL EVEN WHEN IT'S COLD, SO I NEED TO KNOW HOW MANY MAGGOTS HAVE BEEN FEEDING ON A BODY.

FINDING THIS OUT CAN BE DIFFICULT AT TIMES. ANOTHER TYPE OF MAGGOT FEEDS ON BLOWFLY MAGGOTS, REDUCING THEIR NUMBER. COMING UP WITH A DATE FOR WHEN THE EGGS WERE LAID CAN TAKE SOME WORKING OUT!

AT 1:30 P.M. ON SEPTEMBER 25, THE FIRST ADULT BLOWFLIES EMERGED. DR. KRINSKY COULD NOW FIGURE OUT WHEN THE BLOWFLY EGGS WERE LAID.

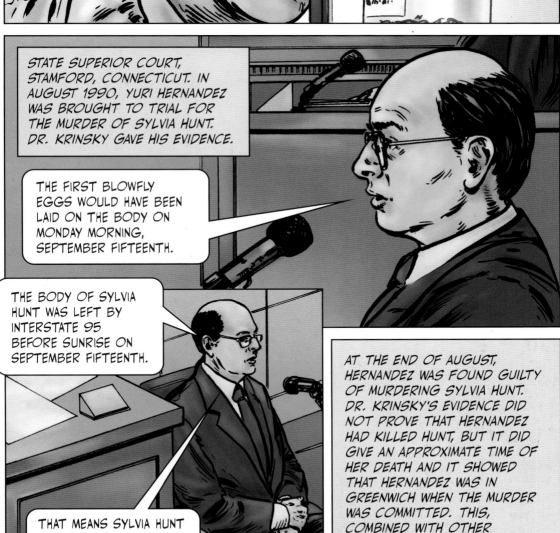

STATE SUPERIOR COURT, STAMFORD, CONNECTICUT. IN AUGUST 1990, YURI HERNANDEZ WAS BROUGHT TO TRIAL FOR THE MURDER OF SYLVIA HUNT. DR. KRINSKY GAVE HIS EVIDENCE.

THE FIRST BLOWFLY EGGS WOULD HAVE BEEN LAID ON THE BODY ON MONDAY MORNING, SEPTEMBER FIFTEENTH.

THE BODY OF SYLVIA HUNT WAS LEFT BY INTERSTATE 95 BEFORE SUNRISE ON SEPTEMBER FIFTEENTH.

THAT MEANS SYLVIA HUNT WAS MURDERED BEFORE THAT TIME AND DATE.

AT THE END OF AUGUST, HERNANDEZ WAS FOUND GUILTY OF MURDERING SYLVIA HUNT. DR. KRINSKY'S EVIDENCE DID NOT PROVE THAT HERNANDEZ HAD KILLED HUNT, BUT IT DID GIVE AN APPROXIMATE TIME OF HER DEATH AND IT SHOWED THAT HERNANDEZ WAS IN GREENWICH WHEN THE MURDER WAS COMMITTED. THIS, COMBINED WITH OTHER EVIDENCE, WAS ENOUGH TO CONVICT HIM.

THE END

THE CASKET MAN

AUGUST 25, 2005, DETROIT, MICHIGAN. TWO POLICE OFFICERS HAD BEEN SENT TO THE POPE FUNERAL HOME TO CHECK OUT A REPORT OF VANDALISM.

THIS PLACE LOOKS LIKE SOMETHING OUT OF A HORROR MOVIE! HOW LONG HAS IT BEEN CLOSED DOWN?

I DON'T KNOW, EIGHTEEN MONTHS OR SO.

IT COULD USE A COAT OF PAINT.

HUH?

HEY, I THINK YOU OUGHT TO COME AND SEE THIS.

SO, YOU'VE FOUND A PAIR OF OLD CASKETS IN A FUNERAL HOME. WHAT'S THE BIG DEAL?

THIS...

...THESE CASKETS AREN'T EMPTY.

NO ONE KNOWS WHY THE BODIES WERE NOT BURIED. THE POLICE BELIEVE THE TWO MEN DIED OF NATURAL CAUSES AND ARE MORE CONCERNED WITH IDENTIFYING THEM FOR NOW.

THIS IS MARC SANTIA FOR WDIV TV-FOUR.

DO YOU THINK WE'LL EVER FIND OUT WHO THEY WERE?

NOT FROM THEIR FACES WE WON'T. YOU SAW WHAT THEY LOOK LIKE—THEY'RE TOO FAR GONE TO BE RECOGNIZED.

"UNKNOWN MALE 142" WAS QUICKLY IDENTIFIED. LEONARD "JUNIOR" SMITH HAD BEEN PUT IN HIS CASKET WEARING A BLUE JUMPSUIT. HIS FAMILY IDENTIFIED HIM FROM ITS DESCRIPTION.

MRS. POPE TOLD US THAT UNCLE JUNIOR HAD BEEN CREMATED.

WE SHOULD HAVE KNOWN SOMETHING WAS WRONG WHEN WE NEVER GOT THE ASHES.

BY MARCH 2006, "UNKNOWN MALE 141" WAS STILL UNCLAIMED AND LYING IN THE WAYNE COUNTY MORTUARY. MEDICAL EXAMINER G.T. JONES DECIDED TO CALL IN OUTSIDE HELP.

THE MICHIGAN STATE POLICE SENT ALONG TROOPER SARAH FOSTER, FORENSIC ARTIST.

I'LL GET SOME PHOTOGRAPHS OF HIM FIRST.

HERE HE IS. AS YOU CAN SEE, HE'S PRETTY SHRIVELED UP.

AND THEN I'M GOING TO NEED THE HEAD.

LATER...

IS THAT THE JOHN DOE?

YES. BEFORE I CAN START WORK ON HIM THE SKULL HAS TO BE CLEAN.

I SCRAPED OFF MOST OF THE SKIN, HAIR, AND FLESH. BOILING WILL GET RID OF THE REST. ANOTHER TWENTY MINUTES SHOULD DO IT.

THE RECONSTRUCTION WAS BEING FOLLOWED BY MARC SANTIA FOR TV STATION WDIV.

THEN WHAT?

THE ANTHROPOLOGISTS GET TO LOOK AT IT.

WHEN THE SKULL WAS COMPLETELY CLEAN, SARAH FOSTER TOOK IT TO SHOW DR. TODD FENTON AT THE MICHIGAN STATE UNIVERSITY ANTHROPOLOGY DEPARTMENT.

FROM THE SHAPE OF THE EYE SOCKETS AND THE NASAL OPENING I CAN SAY THAT HE WAS BLACK. HE WAS ALSO ELDERLY.

SARAH FOSTER'S STUDIO...

THE FIRST THING I HAVE TO DO IS SET THE JAW AT THE RIGHT ANGLE AND PROTECT THE FRAGILE BONES OF THE NOSE AND EYES WITH COTTON AND TAPE.

THESE CHARTS GIVE ME AN AVERAGE THICKNESS OF FAT AND MUSCLE AT VARIOUS POINTS ON THE SKULL.

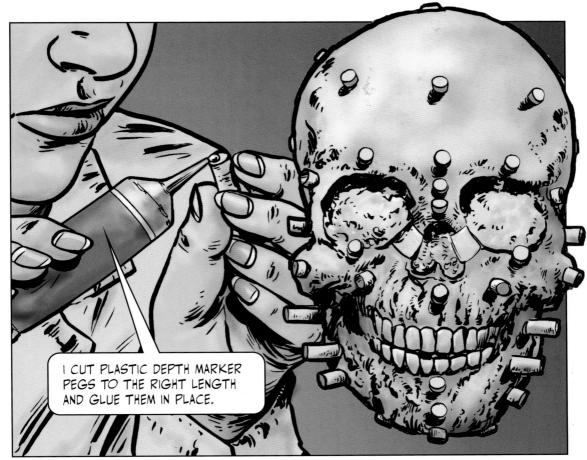

I CUT PLASTIC DEPTH MARKER PEGS TO THE RIGHT LENGTH AND GLUE THEM IN PLACE.

THE DEPTH MARKER PEGS ARE THEN CONNECTED TOGETHER WITH STRIPS OF CLAY. THE PEGS SHOW HOW THICK THE CLAY HAS TO BE.

WHEN THIS IS DONE, I FILL IN THE GAPS BETWEEN THE STRIPS.

ONCE THE RECONSTRUCTION WAS FINISHED THE POLICE HAD FLYERS PRINTED. LATER, WDIV FEATURED THE STORY ON THE EVENING NEWS.

...BUT IF IT HELPS JOG SOMEONE'S MEMORY THEN IT'S BEEN A SUCCESS.

WAYNE COUNTY MORGUE...

EXCUSE ME, I'M HERE ABOUT THE BODY THAT WAS ON THE NEWS LAST NIGHT. I THINK IT'S MY BROTHER, JIMMY. I'VE GOT A PHOTOGRAPH OF HIM HERE.

HE LOOKS JUST LIKE THE MAN ON THE FLYER.

JIMMY LEE ADAMS HAD DIED IN FEBRUARY 2003, AGED 64, BUT DUE TO A MISUNDERSTANDING HE HAD NOT BEEN BURIED. WITHOUT THE SKILLS OF THE FORENSIC ARTIST, THE ADAMS FAMILY WOULD NEVER HAVE KNOWN WHAT HAD HAPPENED TO HIM.

THE END

OTHER FAMOUS CASES

Here are some more celebrated cases that feature forensic anthropology, forensic art, and forensic entomology.

THE CZAR OF RUSSIA'S BONES

On July 16, 1918, Nicholas II, the last czar of Russia, and his family were murdered by soldiers of the revolution. They were buried secretly and in time their graves were forgotten. In 1989 it was announced that their skeletons had been found. The Russian government invited Dr. William Maples, an American forensic anthropologist, to examine the bones. By comparing the skeletons with what was known about the royal family, Dr. Maples showed that the bones belonged to the czar and his family.

THE DISAPPEARED

From 1976 to 1983, Argentina in South America was ruled by army generals who treated their opponents harshly. About 20,000 people were kidnapped, never to be heard of again. They became known as "The Disappeared." When the generals fell from power, forensic anthropologist Clyde Snow was recruited to investigate mass graves that had been found. He and his team managed to identify many of the bodies and found that they had been tortured before being killed. In 1985 his evidence led to six of the nine generals being convicted of murder at their trial.

THE FACE WITH A PAST

In New Jersey in November 1971, John Emil List shot to death the members of his family, drove to the airport, and disappeared. The New Jersey police knew List was the murderer, but the trail went cold. It seemed that List had gotten away with murder. In 1987 the police decided to update List's photograph. They went to forensic artist Frank Bender for help. Bender made a clay bust showing how he thought List might look after 17 years. In 1989 the bust was shown on television. Wanda Flannery noticed how much it looked like her neighbor Bob Clark. She called the police, and Clark was arrested. Fingerprints proved that he was List.

MURDER IN THE PADDY FIELD

Forensic entomology is an old science. There is a story from China, written in 1235 CE, that tells of a murder in a small village. A man had been found, hacked to death in a paddy field. The murderer had used a rice sickle, but since every villager owned one, they all were suspects. When the examining magistrate arrived, he ordered every rice sickle to be placed on a table in the village square. Suddenly, he pointed to one villager and accused him of the crime. The villager confessed. "But how did you know?" he wailed. The magistrate explained. He had watched as flies settled on just one rice sickle, the murder weapon. Even though the sickle had been washed, there were still tiny traces of blood on it, blood that only the flies could sense was there.

GLOSSARY

anthropologist A person who studies humankind.

autopsy An examination of a dead body to discover the cause of death.

bailiff A court official who performs legal duties.

boulevard A wide, tree-lined street in a town or city.

cartilage Flexible tissue that forms bonelike structures in the body.

casket A coffin.

cremated To be burned to ashes.

decaying Rotting.

decomposed Rotted.

elegant Graceful.

guillotine A machine used to behead criminals.

infrared Part of the spectrum that comes after red light but is invisible.

intruder A burglar.

magistrate An officer of the law. Today, a magistrate is a judge in a court of law who deals with minor offenses.

mortuary A funeral home.

pelvis The hip bone.

pupae The stage in blowflies' development when they are enclosed in a protective case, before emerging as a mature insect.

sickle A harvesting tool with a long, curved blade and a short handle.

takings The amount of money made by a business.

thyroid A gland found in the neck.

vandalism Damage done deliberately to property.

FOR MORE INFORMATION

ORGANIZATIONS

American Anthropological Association
2200 Wilson Boulevard, Suite 600
Arlington, VA 22201
Web site: http://www.aaanet.org/aa/index.htm

Forensic Science Center
2825 E. District St.
Tucson, AZ 85714
(520) 243-8600

FOR FURTHER READING

Jackson, Donna, M. *The Bone Detectives: How Forensic Anthropologists Solve Crimes and Uncover Mysteries of the Dead.* New York, NY: Little, Brown & Company, 1996.

Halls, Kelly Milner. *Mysteries of the Mummy Kids.* Plain City, OH: Darby Creek Publishing, 2007.

Maples, William R. and Michael Browning. *Dead Men Do Tell Tales: The Strange and Fascinating Cases of a Forensic Anthropologist.* New York, NY: Broadway Books, 1996.

Scheller, William. *Amazing Archaeologists and Their Finds.* Minneapolis, MN: Oliver Press, 1994.

Shone, Rob. *Graphic Discoveries, Ancient Treasures.* New York, NY: Rosen Publishing, 2008.

Ubelaker, Douglas. *Bones: A Forensic Detective's Casebook.* New York, NY: Doubleday, 1992.

INDEX

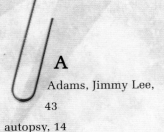

Web Sites

Due to the changing nature of Internet links, Rosen Publishing has developed an online list of Web sites related to the subject of this book. This site is updated regularly. Please use this link to access the list:

http://www.rosenlinks.com/gfs/cosk